THE
BISHOP'S CANDLESTICKS

A Play in One Act

BY
NORMAN McKINNEL

FOUNDED ON AN INCIDENT IN VICTOR HUGO'S NOVEL
"LES MISERABLES"

LONDON
SAMUEL FRENCH, LTD.
PUBLISHERS
26 SOUTHAMPTON STREET
STRAND, W.C.2

NEW YORK
SAMUEL FRENCH
PUBLISHER
28 WEST 38TH STREET

Printing Statement:

Due to the very old age and scarcity of this book,
many of the pages may be hard to read due to the
blurring of the original text, possible missing pages,
missing text, dark backgrounds and other issues
beyond our control.

Because this is such an important and rare work, we
believe it is best to reproduce this book regardless of
its original condition.

Thank you for your understanding.

THE BISHOP'S CANDLESTICKS.

Originally produced at the Duke of York's Theatre on August 24th, 1901, with the following cast:—

THE BISHOP . . . . Mr. A. E. George.
THE CONVICT . . . . Mr. Norman McKinnel.
PERSOMÉ (The Bishop's sister, a widow) . Miss Nannie Griffin.
MARIE . . . . Miss Constance Walton.
SERGEANT OF GENDARMES . . . . . . Mr. Frank Woolfe.

It was revived at the Kingsway Theatre on Friday, December 20th, 1907, with the following cast:—

THE BISHOP . . . . Mr. Henry Vibart.
THE CONVICT . . . . Mr. Lemmon Warde.
PERSOMÉ . . . . Miss Evelyn Hall.
MARIE . . . . Miss Maud Stewart.
SERGEANT OF GENDARMES . . . . . Mr. Douglas Gordon.

TIME.—The beginning of the last century.

PLACE.—France, about thirty miles from Paris.

THE BISHOP'S CANDLESTICKS

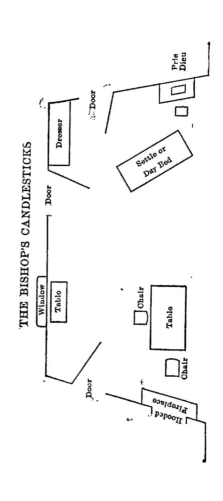

THE BISHOP'S CANDLESTICKS.

SCENE :—*The kitchen of the* BISHOP'S *cottage. It is plainly but substantially furnished. Doors* R. *and* L. *and* L. C. *Window* R. C. *Fireplace with heavy mantelpiece down* R. *Oak settle with cushions behind door* L. C. *Table in window* R. C. *with writing materials and crucifix (wood). Eight-day clock* R. *of window. Kitchen dresser with cupboard to lock down* L. *Oak dining table* R. C. *Chairs, Books, etc. Winter wood scene without. On the mantelpiece are two very handsome candlesticks which look strangely out of place with their surroundings.*

MARIE *and* PERSOMÉ *discovered.* MARIE *stirring some soup on the fire.* PERSOMÉ *laying the cloth, etc.*

PERSOMÉ.   Marie, isn't the soup boiling yet?

MARIE.   Not yet, Madam.

PERSOMÉ.   Well it ought to be. You haven't tended the fire properly, child.

MARIE.   But, Madam, you yourself made the fire up.

PERSOMÉ.   Don't answer me back like that. It is rude.

MARIE.   Yes, Madam.

PERSOMÉ.   Then don't let me have to rebuke you again.

MARIE.   No, Madam.

PERSOMÉ.   I wonder where my brother can be. It is after eleven o'clock (*looking at the clock*) and no sign of him. Marie!

MARIE.   Yes, Madam.

PERSOMÉ.   Did Monseigneur the Bishop leave any message for me?

MARIE.   No, Madam.

PERSOMÉ.   Did he tell you where he was going?

MARIE.   Yes, Madam.

PERSOMÉ.   "Yes, Madam" (*imitating*).   Then why haven't you told me, Stupid!

MARIE.   Madam didn't ask me.

PERSOMÉ.   But that is no reason for your not telling me is it?

MARIE.   Madam said only this morning I was not to chatter, so I thought——

PERSOMÉ.   Ah mon Dieu, you thought!   Ah!   It is hopeless.

MARIE.   Yes, Madam.

PERSOMÉ.   Don't keep saying "Yes, Madam," like a parrot, Nincompoop.

MARIE.   No, Madam.

PERSOMÉ.   Well.   Where did Monseigneur say he was going?

MARIE.   To my mother's, Madam.

PERSOMÉ.   To your mother's indeed!   And why, pray?

MARIE.   Monseigneur asked me how she was, and I told him she was feeling poorly.

PERSOMÉ.   You told him she was feeling poorly, did you?   And so my brother is to be kept out of his bed, and go without his supper because you told him she was feeling poorly.   There's gratitude for you!

MARIE.   Madam, the soup is boiling!

PERSOMÉ.   Then pour it out, fool, and don't chatter. (MARIE *about to do so*) No, no.   Not like that, here let me do it, and do you put the salt cellars on the table—the silver ones.

MARIE.   The silver ones, Madam?

PERSOMÉ.   Yes, the silver ones.   Are you **deaf** as well as stupid?

MARIE.   They are sold, Madam.

PERSOMÉ. Sold! (*with horror*) sold! Are you mad?
Who sold them? Why were they sold?

MARIE. Monseigneur the Bishop told me this after-
noon while you were out to take them to Monsieur
Gervais who has often admired them, and sell them
for as much as I could.

PERSOMÉ. But you had no right to do so without
asking me.

MARIE. But, Madam, Monseigneur the Bishop told
me. (*with awe*)

PERSOMÉ. Monseigneur the Bishop is a—ahem!
but, but what can he have wanted with the money!

MARIE. Pardon, Madam, but I think it was for
Mère Gringoire.

PERSOMÉ. Mère Gringoire indeed. Mère Gringoire!
What, the old witch who lives at the top of the hill, and
who says she is bedridden because she is too lazy to do
any work? And what did Mère Gringoire want with
the money, pray?

MARIE. Madam, it was for the rent. The bailiff
would not wait any longer and threatened to turn her
out to-day if it were not paid, so she sent little Jean to
Monseigneur to ask for help and—

PERSOMÉ. Oh mon Dieu! It is hopeless, hopeless.
We shall have nothing left. His estate is sold, his
savings have gone. His furniture, everything. Were
it not for my little dot we should starve, and now my
beautiful—beautiful (*sob*) salt cellars. Ah, it is too
much, too much (*she breaks down crying*)

MARIE. Madam, I am sorry, if I had known—

PERSOMÉ. Sorry and why, pray? If Monseigneur
the Bishop chooses to sell his salt cellars he may do
so, I suppose. Go and wash your hands, they are
disgracefully dirty.

MARIE. Yes, Madam. (*going towards* R.)

(*Enter the* BISHOP, C.)

BISHOP. Ah! how nice and warm it is in here

It is worth going out in the cold for the sake of the comfort of coming in.

(PERSOMÉ *has hastened to help him off with his coat, etc.* MARIE *has dropped a deep courtesy.*)

BISHOP.   Thank you, dear. (*looking at her*) Why, what is the matter? You have been crying. Has Marie been troublesome, eh? (*shaking his finger at her*) Ah!

PERSOMÉ.   No, it wasn't Marie—but! but!

BISHOP.   Well, well, you shall tell me presently. Marie, my child, run home now, your mother is better, I have prayed with her, and the doctor has been. Run home!

(MARIE *putting on cloak and going.*)

And, Marie, let yourself in quietly in case your mother is asleep.

MARIE.   Oh thanks, thanks, Monseigneur. (*she goes to door* C., *as it opens the snow drives in.*)

BISHOP.   Here, Marie, take my comforter, it will keep you warm. It is very cold to-night.

MARIE.   Oh no, Monseigneur! (*shamefacedly*)

PERSOMÉ.   What nonsense, brother, she is young, she won't hurt.

BISHOP.   Ah, Persomé, you have not been out, you don't know how cold it has become. Here, Marie, let me put it on for you. (*does so*) There! Run along, little one.

(*Exit* MARIE, C.)

PERSOMÉ.   Brother, I have no patience with you. There, sit down and take your soup, it has been waiting ever so long. And if it is spoilt, it serves you right.

BISHOP.   It smells delicious.

PERSOMÉ.   I'm sure Marie's mother is not so ill that you need have stayed out on such a night as this.

I believe those people *pretend* to be ill just to have the Bishop call on them.   They have no thought of the Bishop !

BISHOP.   It is kind of them to want to see me.

PERSOMÉ.   Well for my part I believe that charity begins at home.

BISHOP.   And so you make me this delicious soup. You are very good to me, sister.

PERSOMÉ.   Good to you, yes !   I should think so. I should like to know where you would be without me to look after you.   The dupe of every idle scamp or lying old woman in the Parish.

BISHOP.   If people lie to me they are poorer, not I.

PERSOMÉ.   But it is ridiculous, you will soon have nothing left.   You give away everything, everything ! ! !

BISHOP.   My dear, there is so much suffering in the world, and I can do so little (*sighs*) so very little.

PERSOMÉ.   Suffering, yes, but you never think of the suffering you cause to those who love you best, the suffering you cause to me.

BISHOP (*rising*) You, sister dear.   Have I hurt you ? Ah, I remember you had been crying.   Was it my fault ?   I didn't mean to hurt you.   I am sorry.

PERSOMÉ.   Sorry.   Yes.   Sorry won't mend it. Humph !   Oh, do go on eating your soup before it gets cold.

BISHOP.   Very well, dear. (*sits*)   But tell me——

PERSOMÉ.   You are like a child, I can't trust you out of my sight.   No sooner is my back turned than you get that little minx Marie to sell the silver salt cellars.

BISHOP.   Ah, yes, the salt cellars.   It is a pity.   You, you were proud of them ?

PERSOMÉ.   Proud of them, why they have been in our family for years.

BISHOP.   Yes, it is a pity, they were beautiful, but still, dear, one can eat salt out of china just as well.

PERSOMÉ.   Yes, or meat off the floor I suppose. Oh it's coming to that.   And as for that old wretch

Mère Gringoire, I wonder she had the audacity to send here again. The last time I saw her I gave her such a talking to that it ought to have had some effect.

BISHOP. Yes! I offered to take her in here for a day or two, but she seemed to think it might distress you.

PERSOMÉ. Distress me!!!

BISHOP. And the bailiff, who is a very just man, would not wait longer for the rent, so—so—you see I *had* to pay it.

PERSOMÉ. *You had* to pay it. (*gesture of comic despair*).

BISHOP. Yes, and you see I had no money so I had to dispose of the salt cellars. It was fortunate I had them, wasn't it? (*smiling*) But, I'm sorry I have grieved you.

PERSOMÉ. Oh, go on! go on! you are incorrigible. You'll sell your candlesticks next.

BISHOP (*with real concern.*) No, no, sister, not my candlesticks.

PERSOMÉ. Oh! Why not? They would pay somebody's rent I suppose.

BISHOP. Ah, you are good, sister, to think of that, but, but I don't want to sell them. You see, dear, my mother gave them to me on—on her deathbed just after you were born, and—and she asked me to keep them in remembrance of her, so I would like to keep them, but perhaps it is a sin to set such store by them?

PERSOMÉ. Brother, brother, you will break my heart (*with tears in her voice*). There! don't say anything more. Kiss me and give me your blessing. I'm going to bed. (*they kiss*)

BISHOP (*making sign of the cross and murmuring blessing*)

(PERSOMÉ *locks cupboard door and going.*)

PERSOMÉ. Don't sit up too long and tire your eyes.

BISHOP. No, dear! Good night !

(PERSOMÉ *Exits* R.)

BISHOP. (*comes to table and opens a book then looks up at the candlesticks*) They would pay somebody's rent. It was kind of her to think of that. (*He stirs the fire, trims the lamp, arranges some books and papers, sits down, is restless, shivers slightly, clock outside strikes 12 and he settles to read. Music during this. Enter the* CONVICT *stealthily, he has a long knife and seizes the* BISHOP *from behind.*)

CONVICT. If you call out you are a dead man !

BISHOP. But, my friend, as you see, I am reading. Why should I call out? Can I help you in any way ?

CONVICT (*hoarsely*) I want food. I'm starving, I haven't eaten anything for three days. Give me food quickly, quickly, curse you.

BISHOP. (*eagerly*) But certainly, my son, you shall have food. I will ask my sister for the keys of the cupboard. (*rising*)

CONVICE. Sit down ! ! !

(*The* BISHOP *sits, smiling*)

None of that, my friend! I'm too old a bird to be caught with chaff. You would ask your sister for the keys, would you ? A likely story ! You would rouse the house too. Eh? Ha ! ha ! A good joke truly. Come, where is the food. I want no keys. I have a wolf inside me tearing at my entrails, tearing me ; quick, tell me where the food is.

BISHOP. (*aside*) I wish Persomé would not lock the cupboard. (*aloud*) Come, my friend, you have nothing to fear. My sister and I are alone here.

CONVICT. How do I know that ?

BISHOP. Why I have just told you.

(CONVICT *looks long at the* BISHOP.)

CONVICT. Humph ! I'll risk it.

(BISHOP, *going to door* R.)

But mind! Play me false and as sure as there are devils in Hell I'll drive my knife through your heart. I have nothing to lose.

BISHOP. You have your soul to lose, my son, it is of more value than my heart (*at door* R. *calling*) Persomé, Persome. (*The* CONVICT *stands behind him with his knife ready.*)

PERSOMÉ. (*within*) Yes, Brother.

BISHOP. Here is a poor traveller who is hungry. If you are not undressed will you come and open the cupboard and I will give him some supper.

PERSOMÉ. (*within*) What, at this time of night? A pretty business truly. Are we to have no sleep now? but to be at the beck and call of every ne'er-do-well who happens to pass?

BISHOP. But, Persomé, the traveller is hungry.

PERSOMÉ. Oh, very well, I am coming. (PERSOMÉ *Enters* R., *she sees the knife in the* CONVICT'S *hand*) (*frightened*) Brother, what is he doing with that knife.

BISHOP. The knife, oh, well, you see, dear, perhaps he may have thought that I—I had *sold* ours. (*laughs gently*)

PERSOMÉ. Brother, I am frightened. He glares at us like a wild beast. (*aside to him*)

CONVICT. Hurry, I tell you. Give me food or I'll stick my knife in you both and help myself.

BISHOP. Give me the keys, Persome, (*she gives them to him*) and now, dear, you may go to bed.

(PERSOMÉ *going. The* CONVICT *springs in front of her.*)

CONVICT. Stop! Neither of you leave this room till I do.

(*She looks at the* BISHOP.)

BISHOP. Persomé, will you favour this gentleman with your company at supper. He evidently desires it.

PERSOMÉ. Very well, brother. (*she sits down at table staring at the two*)

BISHOP. Here is some cold pie and a bottle of wine and some bread.

CONVICT. Put them on the table, and stand below it so that I can see you.

(BISHOP *does so and opens drawer in table taking out knife and fork, looking at the knife in* CONVICT'S *hand*).

CONVICT. *My* knife is sharp. (*he runs his finger along the edge and looks at them meaningly*) And as for forks (*taking it up*) Faugh! *steel* (*he throws it away*) We don't use forks in Prison.

PERSOMÉ. Prison?

CONVICT. (*cutting off an enormous slice, which he tears with his fingers like an animal. Then starts*) What was that? (*he looks at the door*) Why the devil do you leave the window unshuttered and the door unbarred so that anyone can come in. (*shutting them*)

BISHOP. That is why they are left open.

CONVICT. Well they are shut now!

BISHOP (*sighs*) For the first time in thirty years.

(CONVICT *eats voraciously and throws a bone on the floor.*)

PERSOMÉ. Oh, my nice clean floor!

(BISHOP *picks up the bone and puts it on plate.*)

CONVICT. You're not afraid of thieves?

BISHOP. I am sorry for them.

CONVICT. Sorry for them. Ha! ha! ha! (*drinks from bottle*) That's a good one. Sorry for them. Ha! ha! ha! (*drinks*) (*suddenly*) What the devil are you?

BISHOP. I am a Bishop.

CONVICT. Ha! ha! ha! A Bishop. Holy Virgin, a Bishop. Well I'm damned!

BISHOP. I hope you may escape that, my son. Persome, you may leave us, this gentleman will excuse you.

PERSOMÉ. Leave you with—

BISHOP. Please! My friend and I can talk more —freely then.

(By this time, owing to his starving condition the wine has affected him).

CONVICT. What's that? Leave us. Yes, yes, leave us. Good night. I want to talk to the Bishop. The Bishop. Ha! ha! *(laughs as he drinks and coughs)*

BISHOP. Good night, Persomé. *(he holds the door open and she goes out R. holding in her skirts as she passes the CONVICT).*

CONVICT. *(chuckling to himself)* The Bishop. Ha! ha! Well I'm—*(suddenly very loudly)* D' you know what I am?

BISHOP. I think one who has suffered much.

CONVICT. Suffered *(puzzled)* suffered? My God, yes. *(drinks)* But that's a long time ago. Ha! ha! That was when I was a man, now I'm not a man; now I'm a number: number 15729 and I've lived in Hell for ten years.

BISHOP. Tell me about it—about Hell.

CONVICT. Why? *(suspiciously)* Do you want to tell the police—to set them on my track.

BISHOP. No! I will not tell the police.

CONVICT *(looks at him earnestly)* I believe you *(scratching his head)*, but damn me if I know why.

BISHOP. *(laying his hand on the CONVICT's arm)* Tell me about the time—the time before you went to— Hell.

CONVICT. It's so long ago I forgot but I had a little cottage, there were vines growing on it *(dreamily)* they looked pretty with the evening sun on them and, and— there was a woman—she was *(thinking hard)*—she must have been my wife—yes. *(suddenly and very rapidly)* Yes, I remember! she was ill, we had no food, I could get no work, it was a bad year, and my wife, my Jeanette was ill, dying *(pause)* so I stole to buy her food. (*long pause the* BISHOP *gently pats his hand*) They caught me.   I pleaded to them, I told them why I stole but they laughed at me, and I was sentenced to ten years in the prison hulks, (*pause*) ten years in Hell. The night I was sentenced the gaoler told me—told me Jeanette was dead. (*sobs, with fury*) Ah, damn them, damn them.   God curse them all (*he sinks on the table sobbing*).

BISHOP.   Now tell me about the prison ship, about Hell.

CONVICT.   Tell you about it?   Look here, I was a man once.   I'm a beast now and they made me what I am.   They chained me up like a wild animal, they lashed me like a hound.   I fed on filth, I was covered with vermin, I slept on boards and I complained. Then they lashed me again.   For ten years, ten years. Oh God!   They took away my name, they took away my soul and they gave me a devil in its place, but one day they were careless, one day they forgot to chain up their wild beast and he escaped.   He was free. That was six weeks ago.   I was free, free to starve.

BISHOP.   To starve?

CONVICT.   Yes, to starve.   They feed you in Hell, but when you escape from it you starve.   They were hunting me everywhere and I had no passport, no name.   So I stole again, I stole these rags, I stole my food daily, I slept in the woods, in barns, anywhere. I dare not ask for work, I dare not go into a town to beg, so I stole and they have made me what I am, they have made me a thief.   God curse them all. (*empties the bottle and throws it into the fireplace* R. *smashing it.*)

BISHOP.   My son, you have suffered much but there is hope for all.

CONVICT.   Hope!   Hope!   Ha! ha! ha! (*laughs wildly*)

BISHOP.   You have walked far, you are tired.   Lie down and sleep on the couch there and I will get you some coverings.

CONVICT.   And if any one comes ?

BISHOP.   No one will come, but if they do, are you not my friend ?

CONVICT.   Your friend ? (*puzzled*)

BISHOP.   They will not molest the Bishop's friend.

CONVICT.   The Bishop's friend. (*scratches his head utterly puzzled*)

BISHOP.   I will get the coverings. (*Exit* L.)

CONVICT. (*looks after him, scratches his head*)   The Bishop's friend ! (*he goes to fire to warm himself and notices the candlesticks. He looks round to see if he is alone and takes them down, weighing them.*)   Silver, by God, and heavy.   What a prize ! (*he hears the* BISHOP *coming and in his haste drops one candlestick on the table.*)

(*Enter the* BISHOP)

BISHOP (*sees what is going on but goes to the settle up* L. *with coverings*)   Ah, you are admiring my candlesticks.   I am proud of them.   They were a gift from my mother.   A little too handsome for this poor cottage perhaps, but all I have to remind me of her.   Your bed is ready.   Will you lie down now ?

CONVICT.   Yes, yes, I'll lie down now. (*puzzled*)   Look here, why the devil are you—ki--kind to me. (*suspiciously*)   What do you want ?   Eh ?

BISHOP.   I want you to have a good sleep, my friend.

CONVICT.   I believe you want to convert me ; save my soul, don't you call it ?   Well it's no good, see ?   I don't want any damned religion, and as for the Church, Bah !   I hate the Church.

BISHOP.   That is a pity, my son, as the Church does not hate you.

CONVICT.   You are going to try to convert me.   Oh, Ha ! ha ! that's a good idea.   Ha ! ha ! ha !   No, no, Monseigneur the Bishop.   I don't want any of your Faith, Hope and Charity, see ?   So anything you do for me you're doing to the devil, understand ? (*defiantly*)

BISHOP. One must do a great deal for the devil, in order to do a little for God.

CONVICT (*angrily*) I don't want any damned religion I tell you.

BISHOP. Won't you lie down now, it is late.

CONVICT (*grumbling*) Well all right, but I won't be preached at, I—I (*on couch*) You're sure no one will come?

BISHOP. I don't think they will, but if they do— you yourself have locked the door.

CONVICT. Humph! I wonder if it's safe. (*he goes to the door and tries it, then turns and sees the* BISHOP *holding the covering, annoyed*) Here! you go to bed. I'll cover myself (*the* BISHOP *hesitates*) Go on, I tell you.

BISHOP. Good night, my son. (*Exit* L.)

(CONVICT *waits till he is off then tries the* BISHOP'S *door*).

CONVICT. No lock of course. Curse it. (*looks round and sees the candlesticks again*) Humph! I'll have another look at them (*he takes them up and toys with them*) Worth hundreds I'll warrant. If I had these turned into money they'd start me fair. Humph! The old boy's fond of them too, said his mother gave him them. His mother, yes. They didn't think of *my* mother when they sent me to Hell. He was kind to me too—but what's a Bishop for except to be kind to you. Here, cheer up, my hearty, you're getting soft. God! wouldn't my chain mates laugh to see 15729 hesitating about collaring the plunder because he felt good. Good! Ha! ha! Oh my God! Good! Ha! ha! 15729 getting soft. That's a good one. Ha! ha! No, I'll take his candlesticks and go, if I stay here he'll preach at me in the morning and I'll get soft. Damn him and his preaching too. Here goes! (*he takes the candlesticks, stows them in his coat and cautiously Exits* L. C. *as he does so the door slams*).

PERSOME (*without*) Who's there? Who's there I

say? Am I to get no sleep to-night. Who's there I
say? (*Enter* R. PERSOMÉ) I'm sure I heard the door
shut (*looking round*) No one here? (*knocks at the*
BISHOP'S *door* L. *Sees the candlesticks have gone*) The
candlesticks, the candlesticks. They are gone.
Brother, brother, come out. Fire, murder, thieves !

(*Enter* BISHOP, L.)

BISHOP. What is it, dear, what is it? What is the
matter?

PERSOMÉ. He has gone. The man with the hungry eyes has gone, and he has taken your candlesticks.

BISHOP. Not my candlesticks, sister, surely not
those (*he looks and sighs*) Ah that is hard, very hard,
I, I—He might have left me those. They were all I
had. (*almost breaking down.*)

PERSOMÉ. Well, but go and inform the police. He
can't have gone far. They will soon catch him, and
you'll get the candlesticks back again. You don't
deserve them, though, leaving them about with a man
like that in the house.

BISHOP. You are right, Persomé. It was my fault.
I led him into temptation.

PERSOMÉ. Oh nonsense ! led him into temptation
indeed ! The man is a thief, a common scoundrelly
thief. I knew it the moment I saw him. Go and inform the police or I will. (*going but he stops her*)

BISHOP. And have him sent back to prison (*very
softly*) sent back to Hell ! No Persomé. It is a just
punishment for me ; I set too great store by them.
It was a sin. My punishment is just but, Oh God, it is
hard, it is very hard. (*he buries his head in his hands*).

PERSOMÉ. No, brother, you are wrong. If you won't
tell the police I will. I will not stand by and see you
robbed. I know you are my brother and my Bishop
and the best man in all France, but you are a fool. I
tell you, a child, and I will not have your goodness
abused. I shall go and inform the police. (*going*)

BISHOP. Stop, Persomé. The candlesticks were mine, they are *his* now. It is better so. He has more need of them than I. My mother would have wished it so had she been here.

PERSOMÉ. But—(*great knocking without*).

SERGEANT (*without*) Monseigneur, Monseigneur, we have something for you, may we enter?

BISHOP. Enter, my son.

(*Enter* SERGEANT *and three* GENDARMES *with* CONVICT *bound. The* SERGEANT *carries the candlesticks.*)

PERSOMÉ. Ah so they have caught you, villain, have they?

SERGEANT. Yes, madam, we found this scoundrel slinking along the road, and as he wouldn't give any account of himself we arrested him on suspicion. Holy Virgin, isn't he strong and didn't he struggle? While we were securing him these candlesticks fell out of his pockets.

(PERSOMÉ *seizes them, goes to table and brushes them with her apron lovingly.*)

I remembered the candlesticks of Monseigneur the Bishop, so we brought him here that you might identify them and then we'll lock him up. (*The* BISHOP *and the* CONVICT *have been looking at each other. The* CONVICT *with dogged defiance.*)

BISHOP. But, but I don't understand, this gentleman is my very good friend.

SERGEANT. Your *friend*, Monseigneur!! Holy Virgin! Well!!!

BISHOP. Yes, my friend, he did me the honour to sup with me to-night and I—I have given him the candlesticks.

SERGEANT (*incredulously*) You gave *him*, *him* your candlesticks? Holy Virgin!

BISHOP (*severely*) Remember, my son, that she is Holy.

SERGEANT (*saluting*) Pardon, Monseigneur.

BISHOP.   And now I think you may let your prisoner go.

SERGEANT.   But he won't show me his papers, he won't tell me who he is.

BISHOP.   I have told you he is my friend.

SERGEANT.   Yes, that's all very well, but—

BISHOP.   He is your Bishop's friend, surely that is enough.

SERGEANT.   Well, but—

BISHOP.   Surely?

(*A pause.   The* SERGEANT *and the* BISHOP *look at each other.*)

SERGEANT.   I—I—Humph! (*to his men*) Loose the prisoner (*they do so*) Right about turn, quick march! (*Exit* SERGEANT *and* GENDARMES.   *A long pause.*)

CONVICT (*very slowly as if in a dream*) You told them you had given me the candlesticks, given me them.   By God!

PERSOMÉ (*shaking her fist at him and hugging the candlesticks to her breast*) Oh you scoundrel, you pitiful scoundrel, you come here and are fed, and warmed, and—and you thieve; steal from your benefactor. Oh you blackguard.

BISHOP.   Persomé, you are overwrought.   Go to your room.

PERSOMÉ.   What, and leave you with him to be cheated again, perhaps murdered.   No, I will not.

BISHOP (*with slight severity*) Persomé, leave us, I wish it.

(*She looks hard at him, then turns towards her door.*)

PERSOMÉ.   Well, if I must go at least I'll take the candlesticks with me.

BISHOP (*more severely*) Persomé, place the candlesticks on that table and leave us.

PERSOMÉ (*defiantly*) I will not!

BISHOP (*loudly and with great severity*) I, your Bishop, command it.

(PERSOMÉ *does so with great reluctance and Exits* R.)

CONVICT (*shamefacedly*) Monseigneur, I'm glad I didn't get away with them, curse me, I am. I'm glad.

BISHOP. Now won't you sleep here, see your bed is ready.

CONVICT. No ! (*looking at the candlesticks*) No ! no ! I daren't, I daren't—besides I must go on, I must get to Paris, it is big, and I—I can be lost there, they won't find me there and I must travel at night, do you understand ?

BISHOP. I see—you must travel by night.

CONVICT. I—I—didn't believe there was any good in the world—one doesn't when one has been in Hell, but somehow I—I—know you're good and, and it's a queer thing to ask but—but could you, would you bless me before I go—I—I think it would help me. I— (*hangs his head very shamefacedly*)

BISHOP (*Makes sign of the cross and murmurs blessing*).

CONVICT (*tries to speak but a sob almost chokes him*) Good night. (*he hurries towards the door*)

BISHOP. Stay, my son, you have forgotten your property (*giving him the candlesticks*).

CONVICT. You mean me—you want me to take them ?

BISHOP. Please, they may help you.

(*The* CONVICT *takes the candlesticks in absolute amazement.*)

BISHOP. And, my son. There is a path through the woods at the back of this cottage which leads to Paris, it is a very lonely path, and I have noticed that my good friends the gendarmes do not like lonely paths at night. It is curious.

CONVICT. Ah, thanks, thanks, Monseigneur. I—I (*he sobs*) Ah ! I'm a fool, a child to cry, but somehow you have made me feel that—that it is just as if something had come into me—as if I were a man again and not a wild beast. (*the door at back is open and the* CONVICT *is standing in it*)

BISHOP (*putting his hand on his shoulder*). Always remember, my son, that this poor body is the Temple of the Living God.

CONVICT (*with great awe*). The Temple of the Living God. I'll remember. (*Exit* L. C.)

(*The* BISHOP *closes the door and goes quietly to the Prie-dieu in the window* R., *he sinks on his knees, and bows his head in prayer.*)

SLOW CURTAIN.

Printed in Great Britain by Butler & Tanner, *Frome and London.*

Printed in the United States
142659LV00005BA